# GUIDES TO RESPONSIBLE HUNTING

# PREPARING FOR YOUR HUNTING TRIP

# GUIDES TO RESPONSIBLE HUNTING

## HUNTING ARMS

## HUNTING SAFETY, LICENSING, AND RULES

## PREPARING AND ENJOYING A MEAL YOU HUNTED

## PREPARING FOR YOUR HUNTING TRIP

## TRACKING AND HUNTING YOUR PREY

# GUIDES TO RESPONSIBLE HUNTING

# PREPARING FOR YOUR HUNTING TRIP

### By Elizabeth Dee

MASON CREST

Mason Crest
450 Parkway Drive, Suite D
Broomall, Pennsylvania 19008
(866) MCP-BOOK (toll-free)
www.masoncrest.com

First printing
9 8 7 6 5 4 3 2 1

ISBN (hardback) 978-1-4222-4101-1
ISBN (series) 978-1-4222-4097-7
ISBN (ebook) 978-1-4222-7700-3

Cataloging-in-Publication Data on file with the Library of Congress

Developed and Produced by National Highlights Inc.
Editor: Keri De Deo
Interior and cover design: Priceless Digital Media
Production: Michelle Luke

**QR CODES AND LINKS TO THIRD-PARTY CONTENT**

You may gain access to certain third-party content ("Third-Party Sites") by scanning and using the QR Codes that appear in this publication (the "QR Codes"). We do not operate or control in any respect any information, products, or services on such Third-Party Sites linked to by us via the QR Codes included in this publication, and we assume no responsibility for any materials you may access using the QR Codes. Your use of the QR Codes may be subject to terms, limitations, or restrictions set forth in the applicable terms of use or otherwise established by the owners of the Third-Party Sites. Our linking to such Third-Party Sites via the QR Codes does not imply an endorsement or sponsorship of such Third-Party Sites or the information, products, or services offered on or through the Third-Party Sites, nor does it imply an endorsement or sponsorship of this publication by the owners of such Third-Party Sites.

# CONTENTS

## KEY ICONS TO LOOK FOR:

**Words to Understand:** These words with their easy-to-understand definitions will increase the reader's understanding of the text while building vocabulary skills.

**Sidebars:** This boxed material within the main text allows readers to build knowledge, gain insights, explore possibilities, and broaden their perspectives by weaving together additional information to provide realistic and holistic perspectives.

**Educational Videos:** Readers can view videos by scanning our QR codes, providing them with additional educational content to supplement the text. Examples include news coverage, moments in history, speeches, iconic sports moments, and much more!

**Text-Dependent Questions:** These questions send the reader back to the text for more careful attention to the evidence presented there.

**Research Projects:** Readers are pointed toward areas of further inquiry connected to each chapter. Suggestions are provided for projects that encourage deeper research and analysis.

**Series Glossary of Key Terms:** This back-of-the book glossary contains terminology used throughout this series. Words found here increase the reader's ability to read and comprehend higher-level books and articles in this field.

## **Words to Understand:**

**rainwear:** Waterproof clothing worn in rainy conditions.

**stamina:** A person's level of endurance and energy.

**thermal underwear:** Underclothing that retains body heat for use in cold weather.

# CHAPTER 1
## PACKING YOUR GEAR

## WHAT WILL YOU TAKE ON A HUNTING TRIP?

What to take on a hunting trip depends on how long the trip will last and how much distance you will travel. Will you be in the woods for one day or camping in the wilderness for two weeks? How far away will you be from a medical facility or a grocery store? These are the sort of questions you should consider when planning for your upcoming hunting trip.

If your hunting trip takes place far from home and convenient shopping, you will need a lot more supplies than for a local trip. You will need a safe water supply, such as bottled water, food for cooking, and shelter from bad weather, such as a tent.

Think about where your hunting trip will take place before packing.

Be careful when choosing your gear.

# CHOOSING CLOTHING AND BOOTS

When planning and packing for a hunt, be sure to take clothing and boots that fit well. Pants, shirts, or jackets that are too small or too large are not only uncomfortable to wear but can be a safety hazard as well. Clothes that don't fit properly can make your movements awkward and clumsy and can cause accidents. Too tight clothing can also restrict your body's blood flow, and you will feel more fatigued than usual.

Boots that don't fit well can cause blisters on long walks and a lot of serious pain for the hunter. Even a hole in a sock can cause a blister or pain by creating friction when walking or hiking. You should choose thick socks to wear with hunting boots that will protect your feet and prevent blisters. Be sure to pack extra pairs of socks to make sure your feet are kept dry to avoid any problems.

If the weather is cold, and you want to wear socks while you sleep, don't wear the same pair you wore all day. Keep your feet clean and dry by changing your socks, and you will keep your feet healthy. Remember, you depend heavily on your feet for traveling during a hunt. Take good care of them.

Make sure to protect your feet from the elements.

Don't make the mistake of wearing a new pair of boots for the first time on a long hunt. Wear the boots for a few days beforehand to make sure they fit well and will not cause any foot pain or blisters. With new clothing, make sure you wash and wear the garments before the hunting trip as well to make sure they will be comfortable and not cause any distractions.

When you are not sure what sort of weather you will encounter during your hunting trip, the best choice for comfort is layering your clothing. When you wear layers of clothes, you can remove a garment if it's a warm day or put it back on when it becomes cooler. By using the layering method, you can remain comfortable no matter what the weather.

## RAINWEAR

You should always plan for rain even if the weather forecast predicts clear skies. Nothing makes a hunting trip more miserable than being wet. Bring a lightweight rain jacket with a hood rolled up tight in your backpack just in case. Waterproof boots are also a good idea. Even if it doesn't rain, you may encounter marshy conditions or the need to cross water while tracking and hunting.

## CAMP STOVE

On long trips, you will need a camping stove to cook food for meals. You can also cook meat you have hunted, such as a rabbit or bird. You can also use a camp stove to fry fish caught in a nearby stream or lake. Be sure to pack cooking oil for frying.

Stoves that operate with fuel canisters are a good choice for camping. Ask an adult to help set up the stove correctly and ignite the fuel. These types of stoves can be very hot to the touch, so be careful not to burn your fingers or set anything on fire. When you finish cooking, be sure to ask an adult to check the stove and make sure it's properly turned off.

Camping stoves such as this one are lightweight and easy to carry.

# GPS OR A COMPASS

When hunting, a GPS is a great tool to prevent you from getting disoriented and lost in unfamiliar territory. If you have a cell phone, it's easy to install a GPS app. Ask your parents for assistance in choosing the right app for your needs. Make sure you know how to use a GPS or compass before you leave on your hunting trip.

Make sure that your cell phone will have service, especially if you are hunting in a remote area with no cell phone towers to boost the signal. It's no use having a GPS app if your phone will not pick up the signal.

You may need a special GPS device if you can't get cell service in the wilderness.

# ROLLING YOUR CLOTHING TO SAVE SPACE

 When packing your clothes for a hunting trip, the smaller you can compress the garments, the less space they will take up in your backpack or duffel bag. Rolling your clothes into a tight roll takes up less space than folding and laying them flat.

Lay out all the items of clothing you want to take on the hunting trip. Separate the clothing into different groups for each day of the trip. This method helps you visually plan what to wear for each day.

In each pile, put a pair of pants, shirt, underwear, and socks you will wear on that particular day. If you think you may need extra clothing because of wet weather or hunting in marshy conditions, include that as well.

Start with the first pile and begin to roll each separate garment into as tight a roll as you can manage. You can also secure the rolled clothes with a rubber band. Pack the rolled garments tightly into your backpack or duffel bag. If you want to be more organized, you can pack the clothes for each day in a single clear plastic bag and label it. The plastic bag will keep the clothes rolled tightly.

Packing a single day's worth of clothing in separate bags will save time that would otherwise be spent rooting around and searching for something to wear. You can also roll and bag any items of clothing to wear for sleeping.

After wearing clothes, you can re-roll them and pack them back in the bag if they are dry. Don't roll and pack any wet or damp clothes or they will mildew. Allow the garment to dry first.

This video shows how to use a stick and the sun to tell directions.

# IMPROVE YOUR STAMINA

Before you go hiking over rough terrain on an extended hunting trip, make sure you are physically in good shape. You will need to rely on the strength of your body to be self-sufficient in the wilderness. Exercising regularly before hunting season starts is an excellent way to make sure you will have the endurance needed to complete the hunt without exhaustion and fatigue.

You can begin your exercise regimen by riding a bike, walking, or participating in sports such as swimming or running. If you have any physical problem, be sure to discuss it with your parents and family doctor before starting any new form of exercise.

Exercising regularly will help build your **stamina** for hunting.

# PLANNING AN EXTENDED HUNTING TRIP IN AUTUMN

Fall weather can be exceptionally mild or freezing. If the weather is warm, don't forget to pack a few items of heavy clothing in case of a cold snap or chilly temperatures at night. A warm sweater and a heavy pair of pants and jacket will provide extra cold-weather protection. You should also make sure you have plenty of blaze orange colored clothing and caps.

Try not to pack more clothing and gear than necessary, especially if you must hike long distances. Traveling light will conserve your strength, and you'll have more endurance. If you find yourself too weighed down with gear and supplies, exhaustion can prevent you from having a successful hunt, or worse, you could have an accident.

Don't forget to pack blaze orange items so other hunters can spot you.

# PERSONAL SUPPLIES:

- An easily erected tent
- A ground cover for the floor of the tent
- A good quality sleeping bag
- **Thermal underwear**
- Heavy socks
- Weather appropriate clothing
- Waterproof boots
- Winter cap with ear flaps if weather is cold
- Regular hunting cap in blaze orange for warmer temps
- Gloves
- Hunting jacket with zip-out lining
- Rainwear such as a lightweight waterproof jacket
- Flashlight
- Extra batteries
- Lighter or matches to ignite campfire
- First aid kit including any prescribed medication
- Snakebite kit
- Pepper spray for protection
- Insect spray
- Water bottle or canteen
- Toothbrush
- Toothpaste
- Toilet paper
- Towels
- Washcloths
- Soap
- Shampoo
- Comb or small hairbrush
- Granola bars, trail mix, or other quick snacks

These are only a few items you'll need for an autumn hunting trip.

# HUNTING SUPPLIES:

- Any necessary hunting permits
- Gun or Bow
- Ammunition
- GPS navigation or compass
- Binoculars
- Camera (if you want photos)
- Supplies for field dressing: knives, saw, paper towels, rope, disposable gloves, plastic bags, assorted sizes of zip ties
- Food
- Water supplies
- Water purification tablets or drops (for an emergency water supply): you must learn how to use these beforehand
- Cooking supplies such as a camping stove and pots
- A separate knife used for food only
- Reflective tacks to mark your trail

If taking your cell phone, make sure it is protected from a harsh environment.

## PROTECTING YOUR CELL PHONE

Your cell phone is a valuable tool for hunting, especially if you get lost in the wilderness and need help finding your way. Make sure you take the necessary steps to protect your phone, so it will work when you need it.

When hunting in a high moisture area such as a swamp, near a lake or stream, or if you get caught in a sudden rainstorm, don't let your cell phone get wet. Using a waterproof bag sold in sports equipment stores can be used to seal your cell phone away from damp conditions. Some bag designs allow you to use the phone without having to remove it.

# PLANNING A SHORT HUNTING TRIP

When you are planning a short trip for a hunt in a rural area, you will need fewer items, but some things should not be left behind, such as a rain jacket, first aid kit, or pepper spray.

**A Hunting Trip of a Day's Duration Should Include:**

- Thermal underwear if weather is cold
- Heavy socks
- Weather appropriate clothing
- Waterproof boots
- Winter cap with ear flaps for cold weather
- Regular hunting cap in blaze orange for warmer temps
- Gloves
- Hunting jacket with zip-out lining
- Rainwear such as a lightweight waterproof jacket
- Flashlight
- Extra batteries
- First aid kit with prescribed medication if needed during the day
- Snakebite kit
- Pepper spray for protection
- Insect spray
- Water bottle or canteen
- Granola bars, trail mix, or other quick snacks

## Hunting Supplies:

- Any necessary hunting permits
- Gun or Bow
- Ammunition
- GPS navigation or compass
- Binoculars
- Camera
  (if you want photos)

- Supplies for field dressing: knives, saw, paper towels, rope, disposable gloves, plastic bags, assorted sizes of zip ties
- Water purification tablets or drops (for an emergency water supply): you must learn how to use these beforehand
- A small sheet of plastic to use in case of rain

# WHAT'S INSIDE YOUR FIRST AID KIT?

You don't know what may happen out in the wild. Stocking your first aid kit with useful items can make your hunt a safer and more comfortable experience.

Every young hunter should consider taking a course in first aid. The American Red Cross and other organizations usually offer these classes free of charge. Knowing what to do in the case of an emergency could save your life or that of other hunters.

If you take any prescription medicines, be sure to include these in your first aid kit. If you use an asthma inhaler, carry it in a zippered pocket on your person so it will be close at hand if you need it. Before going on hunting trips, be sure and discuss the situation with your parents and doctor if you have asthma.

Remember, out in the wild anything can happen and preparation is the key. You don't want to let your medical condition keep you from fun and adventure, but you must take the necessary precautions to ensure your safety.

# ITEMS TO INCLUDE IN YOUR FIRST AID KIT

- Package of assorted band-aids – with several sizes available, you can quickly apply antibacterial ointment and cover the cut or gash to keep out dirt and debris and speed the healing process.

- Antibacterial ointment or spray – covered with a bandage, this medication will prevent infection. Using a spray will be quicker and easier in the field. Be sure to put the spray bottle in a waterproof plastic bag in case it leaks.

- Tweezers – for removing splinters or thorns.

- Scissors – for trimming away small bits of skin around a cut or blister or cutting medical tape.

- Needles – for removing splinters or thorns embedded deeply in the skin.

- Package of sterile gauze pads – to cover a larger cut or abrasion.

- Medical tape

- Rolled bandage

- Antacid

- Pain reliever and fever reducer – for aching, overtired muscles, and fever. Ask advice of parents.

- Hand sanitizer – can be handy after field dressing an animal if no water is available.

- Thermometer

- Eyewash cup and sterile eyewash – use this to remove debris and the occasional insect that can get in your eyes. You will need to store the eyewash in a waterproof plastic bag in case it leaks.

- Any prescribed medications

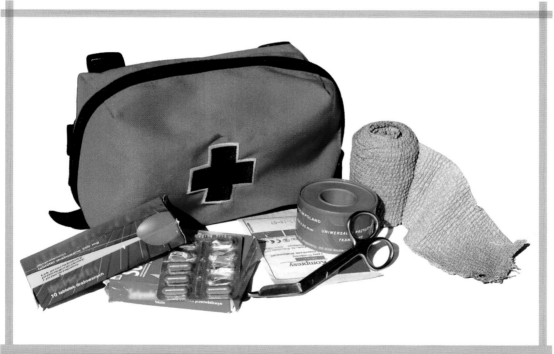

A first aid kit is essential on long and short hunting trips.

# DID YOU KNOW?

Ernest Hemingway was not only a famous writer, but he was also a well-known big game hunter and a world-class fisherman. Hemingway enjoyed the challenge of duck hunting in the United States and stalking big game such as lions, rhinos, and elephants on safari in Africa. Hemingway appreciated the beauty of Africa and referred to the continent as his second home. Learning to shoot and hunt game as a young child, he enjoyed the rugged life of living in the wild and hunting because he felt it brought him closer to nature and to the meaning of life.

Hemingway enjoyed experiencing adventure and danger. One famous photo shows the writer on one knee, smiling broadly beside a big male lion he shot. He escaped death countless times: by surviving two plane crashes, being hit by mortar fire while serving in World War I, and also by recovering from anthrax and malaria.

Hemingway loved fishing and once reeled in a gigantic, record-breaking marlin in 1935. It was the largest fish of its kind ever caught at the time. In the Gulf of Mexico and the Atlantic Ocean, Hemingway also hunted German submarines during World War II using his boat.

Being an accomplished and famous author, Hemingway knew how to tell a good story. The amazing tales of adventure he related in his fiction made his stories very exciting. His own life was just as interesting as his novels. Sometimes, when Hemingway told stories of his experiences to other people, they thought he was either lying or greatly exaggerating!

Hemingway's house in Cuba displays several of the trophy animals he hunted.

## TEXT-DEPENDENT QUESTIONS

1. Why should you not wear new boots for the first time on a hunting trip?

2. Why would a cell phone be needed on a hunting trip?

3. What organization offers free first aid training?

## RESEARCH PROJECT:

You can learn how to calculate the four directions with this low-tech project. First, you will need a straight stick. The stick doesn't have to be perfectly straight, but the straighter, the better. Some people like to use a forked stick. Go outside at night, stick the stick in the ground, and lie down beside it.

Look for the most visible star you can see on the horizon. Don't use a star high in the sky or this method won't work. While lying on your back, line the end of the stick that's pointing upward with the position of the star. If you are using a forked stick, sight the star through the v-shape of the forked stick.

After a few minutes of lying still and watching the star, you will notice that it moves away from the end of the stick or out of the fork. It is the movement of the earth rotating that makes the star appear to move.

Notice which direction the star moves. The direction of star movement will tell you the direction you are facing. Use the following chart as a guide:

Star moves up: the direction you face is east

Star moves down: the direction you face is west

Star moves left: the direction you face is north

Star moves right: the direction you face is south

Try this exercise several times and make a chart of your findings. Use a compass to check the correct directions and see how close are your calculations. Keep practicing with this method until you can develop a reasonable degree of accuracy. Once you learn how to use the stick and star correctly, you can find your way even in the dark.

## Words to Understand:

**live trap:** A trap that captures animals or birds and doesn't kill them.

**nuisance animal:** An animal that invades a house or causes damage to human property.

# CHAPTER 2
## TRAPPING

Humans have set traps for wild animals to provide food and to make fur clothing since prehistoric times. The Native American tribes hunted and trapped animals and taught the settlers how to survive in the hostile environment of the New World.

Trapping is an alternate way to capture an animal or bird without having to stalk and shoot it. In freezing weather, trapping can reduce the time spent out in the snow; plus, a hunter can set multiple traps and catch several animals at one time.

For centuries, traps have been used to catch animals.

# HOW A TRAP WORKS

There are several kinds of traps. Some traps are very simple, and some more complicated, but they all work on the same principle. The bait is placed in a container or within a snare armed with a trigger. When a creature attempts to eat the bait, the trigger is activated, and this causes the trap or snare to close on the animal.

Live traps can be useful for catching nuisance animals such as these raccoons.

# TYPES OF TRAPS

Some traps kill the animal when the trigger is released, such as the simple rat trap. When the rat approaches the bait to eat it, a metal bar slams down on the animal's back, killing it.

**Live traps** are a cage with a door that quickly closes on the animal when it enters the trap. These traps are useful in areas where you might catch someone's pet by mistake. You will be able to release the pet unharmed if they wander into your trap and get caught.

Live traps don't kill animals and are useful for trapping **nuisance animals**, such as a raccoon conducting midnight raids on your trash can or rabbits munching away in your backyard vegetable garden. Once trapped, you can remove the animal back to the wild. In this way, even whole families of nuisance animals can be removed from a human habitat.

Large traps that are used to catch much larger game, such as a "foot-hold" trap, are not suitable for the beginner hunter. These traps snap down on the animal's foot and require more skill to bait and set. Only use such a trap in remote areas where the possibility of capturing a pet is very low. A large animal caught in one of these traps can also be quite aggressive toward the trapper.

# DON'T BE SHY – ASK FOR HELP AND ADVICE

Be sure to ask your parents or an experienced adult hunter to help you choose which type of trap to use for different wildlife and situations, especially if you are a beginner hunter. The right trap is critical to your success and prevents any accidents from happening.

Use simple traps at first that are safe and easy to use. More complicated traps can be dangerous for the beginner to handle and requires a lot of experience to set correctly. Proceed with caution, learning as you go. Be sure to ask plenty of questions and try to understand the mechanism of a trap before you attempt to use it to avoid any possible accidents.

"Foot-hold" traps like these are very dangerous.

# HOW TO AVOID ACCIDENTS WITH TRAPS

When setting a trap, always take your time and don't rush the process. Getting in a hurry to set a trap can cause accidents to happen to your fingers, or the trap can fail to operate correctly.

Always set traps in locations where small children or pets are not likely to have access. You don't want to trap and injure someone's cat, little dog, or child. Small pets wandering in a wooded area can smell the bait and enter the trap just like a wild animal. Even a small snap trap can badly hurt a pet or a small child's foot if they accidentally stumble into the trap.

It's not a good idea to wear gloves when setting a trap. Traps can be tricky to set just right, and gloves can interfere with the dexterity and sensitiveness of one's fingers and cause the trap to fail or cause an accident to the trapper.

Always be careful when setting any trap, and don't be afraid to ask for help.

# BE CAREFUL WHEN RELEASING CAPTIVE WILDLIFE

You will have to be very careful when releasing the animal. A trapped animal, even someone's pet cat or dog, can be very unpredictable or violent. Some wildlife, such as foxes or raccoons can also carry rabies, and you have to be careful not to get bitten or even scratched by these animals. If you are bitten, the animal will have to be tested for rabies to make sure you are not at risk for infection. Rabies can be a fatal disease, so you should always be careful.

Always enlist the help of a parent or responsible adult to help release wildlife. Covering the cage with a tarp is a good idea if the animal is a skunk that could spray, but don't leave the covered cage in the hot sun, or the buildup of heat could kill the animal.

Any animal can become aggressive when trapped.

# WHAT KIND OF BAIT TO USE

Every type of animal and bird has a favorite kind of food. Scavenger animals such as opossums and raccoons prefer smelly bait, and any edible substance that stinks will attract them. A piece of fish or tuna from a can would work well.

Birds like to eat seeds, nuts, or fruits. Some birds also eat bread crumbs, especially pigeons, ducks, and geese. If there are berry bushes in the area bearing fruit, you can pick these and use them as bait. Set your trap far enough from the fruit bushes, so the birds go to your trap and not the bushes. Wild blackberries and blueberries are good examples of fruits to use.

For squirrels, you can use nuts to bait the trap or even a glob of peanut butter. Raw peanuts still in the shell and fruit will work too. When using fruit to trap squirrels, be sure to pick a piece that is overripe and not too green. Fruit that is past its prime will have a stronger aroma that a squirrel can't resist.

Choose your bait carefully. This groundhog was caught using rotting fruit.

Rabbits like any vegetable or fruit, especially if it is out of season and not readily available in the wild. If a hungry rabbit gets a whiff of a piece of cantaloupe in the dead of winter, it will go straight into the trap without much hesitation. Cantaloupe is a good fruit to use for trapping rabbits because it has a pungent smell.

## SCOUT THE AREA FIRST

Before setting your traps, scout the area to see what wildlife is available for trapping. Look for tracks, scat, fur, feathers, or other animal signs. Animal trails or feeding spots are excellent places to set a trap for quick results. You will need to check these traps every day, especially if trapping small animals such as squirrels or rabbits. If these animals are left in a trap too long, a larger animal, such as a coyote, may eat them.

You can leave a piece of fruit or other food tied to a tree or shrub to attract local animals. By examining the tracks left on the ground the next day, you can determine what sort of wildlife came to investigate the food. This information will tell you what type of trap to set and bait to use. Clear the ground of leaves and other debris beforehand to make it easier to observe the tracks and other animal signs.

How to Set a Cage Trap for Raccoons and Opossums.

Scout an area before setting a trap so you know what type of animal you'll catch.

# TRAPPING NUISANCE ANIMALS

Trapping can be a useful skill when it comes to removing wildlife from a home or backyard. Sometimes animals decide to take up residence in an attic, basement, or outdoor shed and create a danger to the home's residents. Raccoons or squirrels in an attic, for instance, can chew on electrical wiring and electrocute themselves, start a house fire, or both.

Some animals, such as a raccoon or large rat, raid garbage cans at night, strewing paper and other litter over the backyard. They can also eat pet food or bird seed. Rabbits can quickly decimate a backyard garden or expensive landscape plants.

Removing these animals from a human habitat can be a challenge. First, study the situation carefully to determine what sort of animal is causing the damage. Search around for bits of fur, scat, or any nesting material the animal used. You should also look for gnawed wood or food debris such as chewed up nut shells.

Small animals, such as squirrels, can bring dead leaves and sticks into an attic space to use as nesting material. This type of debris is a clear sign that squirrels are living and raising their young in the attic. After you have determined what sort of animal you are dealing with, choose a suitable bait for your trap.

For an attic or basement, you can use a trap that doesn't kill the animal, only contains it. Once caught, you can release the animal back into the wild. If you have trapped an animal from a house, don't be tempted to touch it. Be careful not to get bitten or scratched when handling a trap containing an animal.

Many state laws protect wild animals, and it can be illegal to keep one in captivity. Don't try to turn a captured animal into a pet. It could carry an infectious disease that could cause you to become seriously ill. Laws and regulations also dictate whether it is legal to trap certain animals in your area. Ask a parent for help in this matter.

Ask an adult to help you choose a suitable trap for nuisance animal removal and to help you release the creature back into the wild. Be sure to release the animal far enough away from your home so that it doesn't return.

# DID YOU KNOW?

In the 17th century, fur trapping in the northern part of the United States and Canada was big business. European settlers and Native American tribes alike made a good income by trapping wild animals for their fur pelts. Animals like beaver, mink, otter, squirrel, and even moose were in demand for hats, coats, and other articles of fashionable clothing worn in Europe, and many companies were eager to buy fur pelts from the trappers.

Fur trading used to be a big business in the United States and Canada.

One company, known as the Hudson's Bay Company, was started by several entrepreneurs to acquire the fine furs of North America. The company sold the high-quality pelts to the European furriers that manufactured the hats and clothing. The company established trading posts at different points along the Great Lakes where trappers could come to trade their fur pelts for useful items such as blankets, woolen blankets, knives, or cooking pots.

As time went by, more trading posts were established to accommodate the increasing flow of animal pelts supplied by the trappers to the European furriers. The Hudson's Bay Company flourished and eventually grew into a huge business.

The European and Native American trappers that supplied the pelts for the fur trading companies worked through the bitterly cold fall and winter seasons to collect and preserve as many furs as possible. When the spring thaw finally arrived, the trappers would make their way by boat or by foot to the trading posts to sell the beautiful furs.

As time passed, European fashions changed and items made from animal fur fell out of favor. Men didn't want to wear tall beaver hats anymore. Settlers moving into the region began to diminish the available animals that the trappers harvested for their fur. The Hudson's Bay Company issued false rumors that the northern land was not suitable for agriculture, but the wagon trains and pioneers still came, and eventually, large portions of the wilderness became settled.

Traps have evolved over the years to be more humane.

## TEXT-DEPENDENT QUESTIONS:

1. Why should a beginner not attempt to use a large trap?

2. Why should you scout an area first before setting a trap?

3. What type of bait would you use for a trap to catch a squirrel?

## RESEARCH PROJECT

Start this project by studying the basic principles of a trap. Draw a simple diagram of a trap intended to capture a small animal or bird. Research what sort of bait is the best for this type of trap and for the creature you want to catch.

The next step is to build the trap using simple low-cost or free materials. You will want this trap to be as low-tech as possible.

With the advice and guidance of an adult, experiment with the trap in a place where you will not capture pets or endanger small children. For this reason, you want to trap the animal and not kill it, so make a live trap. Use the trap several times to better understand the process and keep a record of your successes and failures. How can you improve the trap? Use several types of bait and see which one works the best.

Be sure to check the trap every day so no animal will die of starvation or dehydration. Release all animals you catch in the trap.

Write a two-page report on your results and present it to three experienced trappers or hunters. Ask them for feedback. If you keep a hunting journal, record all your findings for future reference.

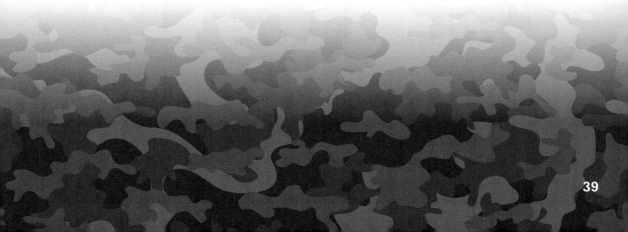

 **Words to Understand:**

**bear pole:** A pole used to hang food or trash so a bear can't reach it.

**bushcraft:** The knowledge and ability to survive in the wilderness by hunting, trapping, finding water, and foraging.

**kindling:** A soft wood for starting a fire.

# CHAPTER 3
## CAMPING SKILLS

## IMPORTANT BUSHCRAFT SKILLS

With overnight or long-term hunting trips, it's helpful to have camping and survival skills. You need to know how to avoid hazardous situations and survive in wild surroundings, and **bushcraft** skills can help you accomplish this. Bushcraft knowledge is essential and can save your life.

Going into the wilderness, even for a few hours, can expose the young hunter to a lot of potential dangers. Coming face to face with aggressive wild animals, stinging insects, freezing temperatures, poison ivy, or the threat of getting lost or exposed to a dangerous disease like rabies can threaten the safety and personal comfort of the hunter.

Learning some basic survival skills can help you on your hunting trip.

You need to know what you are doing to stay safe in a wild environment, and learning necessary survival skills can help. Once you learn the basics of bushcraft, you can build on this knowledge, and with experience, you can hone your skills as well as learn new ones.

# HOW TO BUILD A CAMPFIRE

Campfires can provide warmth, light, and a place to cook your food. You don't want to neglect to master this essential skill.

First, locate an appropriate place to build your fire. Ideally, you need a clear space not too near any trees, bushes, or tall grass. It helps to dig a small pit for the fire, especially if you want to use the fire for cooking, but if you don't have a shovel or spade handy, omit this step. Gathering some good-sized stones and piling them around the fire helps keep the flames from spreading into the underbrush.

Once you've made a stone circle, now is the time to gather firewood and **kindling**. For kindling, search around on the ground for older, softer wood and very small twigs that will ignite quickly.

Never use green wood for kindling because it doesn't burn as well as seasoned, older wood. You can burn green wood once you have gotten the fire going, especially if you want it to burn slower and longer.

Gather some dead leaves and grass, too. Make a small pile of them in the center of your stone circle, and then begin to layer the kindling over the leaves and grass. Don't lay the kindling directly on top of the leaves, but prop it against the sides of the leaf pile to make a teepee-like shape. Layer the smallest twigs first and then the pieces of dead wood. Don't use big twigs now, only the smallest you can find.

After your kindling is ready, start to layer some larger sticks over the small twigs. Don't use too many sticks at this time. You want the center of the pile to get plenty of oxygen so it will burn well.

To build a fire, start with small wood placed in a teepee style.

# IGNITING THE FIRE

When your teepee of sticks is ready, it's time to light the fire. There are several ways to do this. The simplest way is to use a lighter or matches. Other ways include using a glass magnifying lens, flint, steel, or friction with two sticks. Of the other methods, the magnifying lens is probably the most reliable and the easiest way to produce flame if there is sunshine. A magnifying lens is small and lightweight, and it won't take up much space in your backpack. Using the lens in strong sunlight will produce a flame in just a few seconds.

Some compasses have a small magnifying lens embedded in the handle, and that's useful for starting fires. When purchasing a compass for camping, be sure to get one with the magnifying lens and you will always have an alternate way to start a campfire.

If you plan to use a lighter, bring several because they can be unreliable, especially in damp conditions. If you are camping and the one lighter you brought with you fails, you'll spend a cold, dark evening. Always pack some waterproof matches as a backup.

When the fire starts to burn and grow hotter, you should continue to add more sticks. When the flames are hot and bright, you can begin to add green wood mixed with the dry sticks so the fire will burn longer with less fuel.

If you want to cook food, let the fire burn down, and use the coals. Trying to cook over a flame is not recommended because the temperature will be too hot and will burn the food.

Building a campfire is an essential hunting skill.

You want to keep bears far away from your camp, so take every precaution.

## IF IT SMELLS GOOD...BE CAREFUL!

When camping, you need to be careful with substances that have a pleasant smell, such as deodorant, perfume, or toothpaste or even bottles and cans of soda. Sweet-smelling fragrances will attract all sorts of wildlife from stinging insects to bears. When camping, it's best to use non-scented products. After drinking bottled soda, rinse the cup immediately, and if you are drinking from a can or small bottle, put it in the trash and hang it from a tree or bear pole.

When using a flavored commercial toothpaste to brush your teeth or mouthwash for dental care in camp, make sure you spit into the trash bag you hang in the tree. Don't spit out the product out onto the ground. It's best, however, to use a non-scented, biodegradable product that won't attract wildlife.

# STORING FOOD SAFELY

Small animals or birds may attempt to steal your food and be a general nuisance, but bears that want to eat your supplies can create a life-threatening situation. Bears are not only cunning, but they are also powerful and have a very keen sense of smell. They have been known to rip their way into cars to get a sugary treat like donuts or cookies.

If you are camping in bear territory, you'll need a bear canister to store your food safely. These containers are made of hard plastic and are difficult for bears to open. A very intelligent animal, bears have learned over the years that it's almost impossible to open these canisters and usually leave them alone. If the bears can't get any food from your supplies, they will not waste their time hanging around your camp.

Another advantage to using bear canisters is that you don't have to keep your food hanging from a tree or a **bear pole** where it can be hard to hoist the supplies down and back up when you want to prepare a meal. You can leave the bear canister sitting on the ground.

Food lockers made of metal can also work to keep animals including bears out of your food supplies, but you have to be careful with these containers. If you forget to secure the latch correctly and firmly each time you use the food locker, a bear can get in and eat your supplies.

A bear cannister like this one will keep bears away from your food and your camp.

# TRASH DISPOSAL

When camping for an extended period, you will need to have a system to deal with your trash, including leftovers from your hunting or fishing, such as animal carcasses or fish remains. Bears and raccoons are notorious for rooting through garbage and making a giant mess in your camp in the middle of the night.

After you have eaten a meal, you will need to deal with the leftovers and not leave them lying about to attract insects or other wildlife to your camp. If you are using paper plates, toss the whole thing into a designated trash bag or scrape the contents of a regular plate into the plastic bag. Wash the plate well afterward with soap and lay it out to dry.

Put any empty cans, food containers, egg shells, vegetable peelings, or bacon grease into the bag as well, and hang the bag up in a tree or use a bear pole. If you accumulate a lot of trash while camping, you'll need to use several bags to hold it all.

One way to deal with excess garbage is to remove packaging from items before you leave home. Take food out of outer boxes and only take the inner contents. For example, if you have a box of granola, only take the inner bag and leave the box.

When field dressing an animal, it's better to leave the remains of the carcass far from your camp rather than transport it back to camp. Any part of a dead animal will attract bears and other animals to your camp, usually while you are asleep!

Some campgrounds will have designated bearproof trash bins.

# SET UP A TOILET AREA

Human urine and fecal matter can also attract insects and other wildlife to your camp as well as contaminate any nearby water, such as a stream. If you are camping for an extended period in one area, you may want to dig a trench to handle your urine and feces. Make sure you choose an area where there's no poison ivy nearby.

Don't locate the trench close to camp, but not too far away either. Anytime you need to visit the trench, cover the results afterward with dirt. With each visit, you can work your way down the trench, and if you need more room, just dig the trench longer or make another one.

Using a trench for your toilet will allow the urine and feces to break down and return to the earth. If you need to use toilet paper, bury it in the trench, and it will eventually decompose as well.

# FINDING YOUR WAY

It's very easy to become disoriented in the wilderness. Humans have become accustomed to being guided by road signs and maps when living in civilization. Out in the wild, beyond cities and towns, road signs do not exist, so a young hunter must depend on their senses to navigate the terrain.

Getting lost in the wilderness is a real possibility if you're unprepared and untrained.

A young hunter should take the time to train themselves to be very observant of their surroundings at all times when in the wild. You can even leave signs to mark your trails, such as strips of colored plastic or reflective tacks bought for this purpose.

# USING REFLECTIVE TACKS

This product is a tack with a reflective head that you can easily stick into the bark of trees. Leaving a trail of these tacks can help you find your way in unfamiliar terrain, especially a thick forest, and it doesn't harm the tree. In the dark, these tacks will reflect the light of a flashlight.

Reflective tacks are a valuable tool for the young hunter. They're small and easy to carry in your backpack. They are also inexpensive to buy at most sports stores.

# HUNT IN A GROUP

A beginning hunter should always hunt in a group. More people together can mean safety in the wild. If you become lost, your companions will come looking for you. If they can't find you, someone will eventually call for help, and the professionals will start searching for you.

Getting lost can be a scary situation. Your mind races with frightening thoughts and stories you've heard about other people getting lost. You tend to panic and rush off in any direction.

Hunting in a group helps keep you safe.

If you're lost in the woods, stay calm, light a fire, and stay where you are.

# STAY CALM!

The first thing to do if lost is to remain calm. Don't panic! You need to think and make logical decisions. Even if it is growing dark, just rest a bit and try to determine if any part of the landscape looks familiar or if you can remember the way back to camp.

If you have no clue where you are, just sit tight and wait. When your fellow hunters realize you're missing, they will search or call for help if they can't find you. Stay in the general area.

If you are near a hill or other high spot, climbing to the top may help you see further and possibly figure out your location. If you can climb a tree without injuring yourself, this can help you see into the distance and perhaps determine your position.

If you get lost with a group, follow the same guidelines as above. Make sure everyone stays together by reminding them when it comes to wild animals, there is safety in numbers for humans.

Get busy and start a fire because smoke can alert searchers to your location. If at any time you hear other people shouting in the distance, try firing your gun to signal them. Ordinarily, you should not shoot into the air, but this is an emergency.

# A SHEET OF PLASTIC AND FIRE IN THE RAIN

 If you carry a sheet of plastic in your backpack, you can use it in case of sudden, heavy rain. Drape the plastic over your head to keep the rain from soaking your clothing.

If you become lost in the woods, the sheet of plastic has many uses. You can use it when sleeping to avoid lying on damp, cold ground which can cause hypothermia. The plastic can also be used to make a small emergency lean-to by propping the front half up with sticks and using rocks to keep the back edge on the ground. This will create a v-shaped space you can crawl in for shelter from the rain.

If you are lost and want to build a fire in the rain, you can suspend your plastic sheet overhead and build a fire underneath. Even if the sticks are wet, you can use a knife to whittle or shave off thin pieces of wood that will be dry underneath the wet exterior. Use these shavings for kindling and to get your fire started. Once you get a small fire started, you can lay pieces of wood close to the fire, and the heat will dry them. Once they are dry, you can lay them on the fire to burn.

An alternative to wood shavings is to carry a small plastic bag of dryer lint to use as kindling, in case you need to start a fire in the rain. Lint works exceptionally well when starting a fire.

Some sports stores sell survival kits for hunters in case they get lost. These kits are compact and don't take up much room in a backpack.

Dryer lint can be excellent starter fuel for a campfire.

# FIND FOOD AND WATER

Every young hunter needs to know how to find edible plants in the wild. That way, if you get lost, you will not starve. The best way to find out which plants are safe and which ones are toxic is to ask a parent to arrange some classes for you on the subject or someone to give you one-on-one instruction. The information you learn may prove beneficial one day.

Water purification tablets can make water safe to drink in the wild. Make sure you know how to use these tablets before going into the wild. Ask a parent or a knowledgeable adult to help you with this issue before you go hunting.

# DID YOU KNOW?

There are many stories of kids getting lost in the wilderness and surviving by foraging for food and drinking creek water. Some found wild berries to eat while others ate only the plants they recognized as edible.

Distracted by photographing nature scenes in Florida, an eleven-year-old girl got lost in the dangerous swamps of that region, surrounded by alligators and poisonous snakes. However, she survived for four days by eating plants she recognized and sleeping inside a hollow log for shelter. The girl later said she sang songs to help her stay calm so she could make good decisions about what to do next to stay alive.

A nine-year-old boy on a fishing trip at a lake in Utah got lost while trying to find his way back to camp. He survived by relying on bushcraft skills he learned from watching a tv show. He used nearby natural materials for a shelter and used his rainproof clothing for wind and rain protection.

Another young boy also got lost in the mountains of Utah on a Boy Scout trip, and he survived by eating mint leaves growing nearby as well as drinking water from a creek. He was found unharmed after a few days.

In the Australian Outback, a teenager left his home and entered the wilderness during a period of intense and deadly heat. In spite of the high temperatures, he managed to stay alive by catching fish in a creek and eating them for over two months.

A father and his thirteen-year-old son survived freezing temperatures in Australia for several days by building a small shelter from the natural materials they found nearby. The pair had gotten lost while on a hike through the region.

This Swiss video shows a lot of useful bushcraft techniques such as using wedges of wood to split logs, making kindling, and how to start a fire for cooking and warmth.

Using your wits and survival skills, it is possible to survive in the wilderness.

## TEXT-DEPENDENT QUESTIONS:

1. What's the correct way to make a fire?

2. Why should you not use a flaming fire for cooking?

3. What's the first thing to do if you become lost in the wild?

## RESEARCH PROJECT:

On the Internet, search for different ways to make a small and simple shelter, such as a lean-to, for use when hunting. Make several diagrams of how to build such a shelter and list what materials you would use from nature. Research what is the quickest, easiest, and most efficient way to build a lean-to with local materials. Investigate how to build a structure that will help conserve body heat in an emergency.

For the next step, construct a simple lean-to in your backyard or at a friend's house from natural materials. Be sure to get a parent's permission first.

Write a three-page paper on your project. Present this report to your friends and fellow hunters.

 **Words to Understand:**

**muscle memory:** When a person's muscles can make an automatic movement without thinking about it because of a lot of practice.

**plinking:** Target practice with a small gun.

# CHAPTER 4
## PRACTICE

## WHY YOU NEED TO PRACTICE

Regular practice of all hunting skills will help a beginner hunter become a better shot and more accomplished in bushcraft. The more time and effort you put into practice, the more you will sharpen your skills and the better hunter you will become.

Whether you choose to practice at a shooting range or in your backyard if you live in a rural area, keep practicing if you want to become an accomplished hunter. Every sport takes lots of practice, and learning to shoot well is no exception. Whether you are **plinking** in your backyard or out in the wild shooting for practice, just keep working toward your goal of achieving a better aim and becoming a better hunter.

Practicing in a controlled environment will help you when it's time for hunting.

# PRACTICE FOR BEGINNERS

Beginning hunters should spend as much time as possible handling their weapon without ammo. Getting to know the feel, the weight, and the contours of the gun or bow helps when it comes time to learn how to shoot. In the beginning, practice walking around with your weapon with an adult who can show you how to hold it correctly. Learn how to walk and carry your weapon safely during a hunt as well as how to transport it safely.

Practicing cleaning a gun will help a beginner to get to know the inside and outside of their weapon. Knowing the interior parts of a gun helps a beginner to understand better how the mechanism works.

When beginners become familiar with the feel of their weapon, they can begin to practice loading and unloading the ammunition. Practice until you can load a gun quickly and smoothly without fumbling or dropping anything. Mastering loading and unloading your gun quickly and efficiently is crucial when you must perform this action in a hurry while hunting.

# PRACTICE FOR THE MORE EXPERIENCED HUNTER

Even a more experienced young hunter can benefit from practicing cleaning and loading a gun. The more you handle a weapon with your hands, the more of an expert you become with that weapon. Over time, your hands become very familiar with the "feel" of that particular firearm, and you develop **muscle memory**. The same is true for a bow.

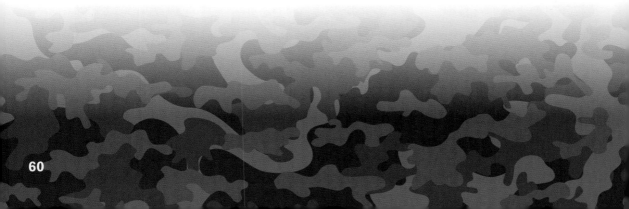

Lots of target practice will make you a better hunter.

# WHAT HAPPENS WHEN YOU PRACTICE

The practice of frequently handling your weapon, as well as target shooting, can teach you many things. First, you learn the art of concentration. When you are aiming your gun or arrow, you must focus intently on what you are doing to make the shot an accurate one. You need to focus on your **stance**, the placement of the weapon, and how steady your arms are all simultaneously.

Just before a shot, concentrate on where the ammunition or arrow will hit the target. Focus your eyes intently on the crosshairs of the gun's sight and aim carefully.

Practicing will also teach you how to hold your body as steady as possible. Holding the body absolutely still may be a difficult achievement for the youngest hunters, but with practice, they will improve.

# DON'T GIVE UP!

An essential part of weapon practice is not becoming discouraged and giving up. Sure, learning to shoot a weapon and hunting is overwhelming at first with so many rules and new things to learn. However, it will get easier the more you practice and learn. Over time, you will figure out how to handle your weapon more skillfully, and your shot accuracy will improve.

If your shot accuracy doesn't improve as fast as you would like it to, don't worry. Have patience with yourself. Just keep at it and practice more. Don't compare yourself to your friend or sibling that's a really good shot already. Everyone is different, and we all learn at different speeds. Give yourself the time you need to learn and develop accuracy.

Everyone has good and bad days when it comes to accuracy with a weapon and hunting. Some days it will seem like you can't hit the side of a huge building with a bullet or arrow, and then on other days, every shot will be perfect. Don't judge yourself too harshly on the bad days. Just know they will pass and tomorrow is another chance to improve your skills.

Practicing your stance is extremely important in learning to shoot well.

Keeping a hunting journal can also help you learn what worked and what didn't.

# THE HUNTING JOURNAL

One of the things you can do to improve your hunting skills is to keep a journal. In a journal you can record all of the new information that you learn about hunting and bushcraft as well as your own opinions and insights. Keeping a written record of all of your successes and failures will help you learn from your past mistakes. It can also help you to form your strategies of shooting and hunting.

When your past learning experiences are written down, you will be able to go back months or even years later and re-examine why you failed or why you succeeded. For instance, when learning how to trap animals, you can keep detailed records of the bait and method of trapping used and if it worked well or not.

Keeping a written record will help you track your progress as a hunter as well as plan future goals. You can write down all of the advice you've gotten from other, more experienced hunters so you won't forget over time. That way, even if your mentors eventually pass from your life, you will still have their words of wisdom to guide you. When you keep a journal, you can review over again what your grandfather taught you about squirrel hunting when you were eight years old and continue to learn from his experience.

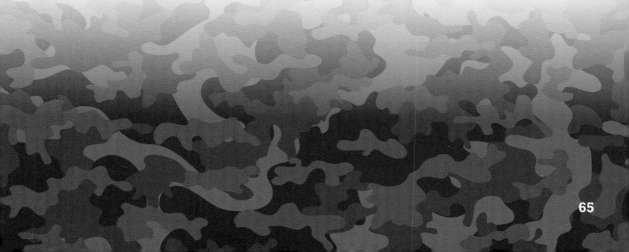

# THE DIFFERENT KINDS OF TARGETS

When you practice shooting, use paper targets. With paper, you can see exactly where the bullet or arrow passed through the surface. Being able to see how close or far off the mark you hit can help improve your aim. It can also help you refine your technique.

You can also draw special targets on a long roll of paper purchased at craft stores. You can create any image you like to use for practice.

A newer kind of target is the splatter targets constructed of a unique substance that forms a white ring around where the bullet enters, making it easy to see. Splatter targets are visible from a distance, so you don't have to get close to see the bullet hole. You can purchase these targets in all sorts of fun images such as monsters, aliens, or even zombies to liven up your practice sessions.

Keeping a hunting journal can also help you learn
what worked and what didn't.

On some targets, the bullseye is yellow instead of red.

# OTHER ACTIVITIES TO HELP YOU BECOME A BETTER HUNTER

There are other ways you can improve your hunting skills besides target practice. Talking with older and more experienced hunters about better and more efficient ways to hunt is one way to learn. These skilled hunters can share valuable tips and tricks to help you become a better hunter. Listen carefully to what they have to teach you.

You can learn a lot about how animals behave simply by observing wildlife.

You can spend time sitting in deer stands or blinds and watching the wildlife. You can learn a lot about the ways and habits of animals and birds by observing them in secret. The more you learn about the creatures, the better hunter you can become.

This short video from the National Shooting Sports Foundation covers firearm safety and etiquette at the indoor shooting range.

## FRIENDLY COMPETITION CAN ADD ENTHUSIASM

Finding a friend who shares your drive to become a better hunter can create friendly competition and help you achieve your goals. A family member such as a sibling can also be your challenger.

Practicing with a competitor can be fun and exciting, especially if you make your target shooting into a contest. Think up some prizes for the winner, such as a special treat. For example, if your friend wins, you will buy him or her an ice cream or vice versa.

Don't get angry and try not to feel frustrated if you lose a round of target practice. Don't act superior to the loser if you win! Keep your attitude friendly and just concentrate on having fun. While you are having fun, your shooting skills will also continue to improve.

With your buddy, watch instructive videos and TV programs together and mutually discuss ways to improve each other's strengths and overcome any weaknesses. Let your friendly rivalry work for you and your buddy and not against you.

Join any shooting or archery competitions available in your area. Even if you don't win, being able to observe more experienced shooters in action can teach you a lot about the sport. Also, you may get some valuable tips and pointers from the experts that will improve your accuracy and form.

Summer camps that teach intensive courses on archery or good marksmanship can also help you improve your shooting skills. Search on the Internet for any local camps in your area, and ask your parents for permission to attend.

# PRACTICE SHOOTING IN THE WILD

Shooting in the wild can help you develop a knowledge of the land and the type of terrain you will be dealing with on a hunt. For example, if you will be hunting in a dusty area of low scrub bushes and bright sunlight, that is where you should practice shooting so you can become accustomed to the conditions. Become comfortable with your surroundings, and you will know what to expect when you hunt there.

If you are familiar with that scrubby hunting area, you'll expect the dust that gets in your eyes and throat to cause you to cough. You'll know to bring a bandana to tie around the bottom of your face to keep out the dust. Keeping the dust out of your throat will stop you from coughing and alerting the wild game in the area. No coughing means a more successful hunt.

## DID YOU KNOW?

There is probably no hunter, pioneer, and explorer more famous than Daniel Boone. Boone became a legend in his own time and was well known for his daring exploits. According to popular stories, he was a master hunter, trapper, and an unrivaled expert when it came to bushcraft. Boone loved hunting all his long life as well as living in the wild.

Daniel Boone (1734-1820). This engraving of Daniel Boone was created by J.B. Longacre in 1835.

One of the first settlers in Kentucky, Boone was captured by the Shawnee tribe, and in 1776, his daughter, Jemima, was kidnapped by members of the same tribe. Boone led a rescue party that tracked the kidnappers for two days and rescued Jemima along with two other girls. Several years later, the Shawnee would kill his brother Ned as well as Boone's two grown sons in battle.

In 1784, John Filson wrote a book about Daniel Boone, which described many of his exciting adventures. The book was first published in Europe and later in the United States, spreading Boone's fame far and wide. Even the English poet, Lord Byron, wrote complimentary stanzas about Daniel Boone, the backwoodsman who hunted deer and bears and was a happy man.

## TEXT-DEPENDENT QUESTIONS:

1. Why is target practice so important?
2. Why should a young hunter practice handling their weapon before learning how to shoot?
3. How can a hunting journal help you become a better hunter?
4. What other activities can improve your hunting skills besides target practice?
5. Why should you join shooting or archery competitions?

## RESEARCH PROJECT:

To do this project, you will need six paper targets for practice, a weapon of your choice, ammunition or arrows, and your parents' permission.

On the first sunny day, set a target up for practice in the early morning hours when the sun is still low on the horizon. Observe the weather conditions and record them in your hunting journal. Is there fog in the air? Is the sun bright, or is the sky overcast and dark? Practice with ten shots and record the results in your journal.

At noon, if the sun is high, practice again with another ten shots and a fresh paper target. If the day is overcast, wait until another day when the sun is shining. Practice with the ten shots and record your results. Don't forget to record the weather conditions in your hunting journal. Is the wind blowing? Is the day cooler or warmer? Did you have different results?

In the late afternoon when the sun is slanting from the west, repeat the process with a fresh paper target. After you have practiced, analyze the information you have recorded. Did the weather conditions affect your aim? How about the rays of the sun? Did the slant of the early morning sun affect your aim? How about the late evening sun?

Repeat this whole process from start to finish so you will have two complete days of target practice to analyze. See if you can determine the best time of day and weather conditions for you to target practice. When is your aim the most accurate?

Record all of your findings in your hunting journal or write a two-page report. It will be more useful to keep a journal, however. Discuss your experiment with at least three experienced, seasoned hunters. Record their opinions in your journal for future reference.

**Briars:** A patch of thick underbrush that is full of thorny bushes. Rabbits and other small game love to hide in these.

**Burrow:** A hole made by a small animal where they live and stay safe from predators. It is also the word for what an animal does when it digs these holes.

**Carcass:** The dead body of an animal after the innards have been removed and before it has been skinned.

**Field dress:** To remove the inner organs from an animal after it has been harvested. It's important to field dress an animal as quickly as possible after it has been harvested.

**Habitat:** The area in which an animal lives. It's important to preserve animal habitats.

**Hide:** The skin of an animal once it has been removed from the animal. Hides can be made into clothing and other useful gear.

**Homestead:** A place or plot of land where a family makes their home. This is different from habitat because it is manmade.

**Kmph:** An abbreviation for kilometers per hour, which is a metric unit of measurement for speed. One kilometer is equal to approximately .62 miles.

**Marsh:** A wet area of land covered with grasses. The water in a marsh is often hidden by cattail, grasses, and other plants.

**Maul:** To attack and injure—either an animal or human being can be mauled.

**Mph:** An abbreviation for miles per hour, which is a unit of measurement for speed. One mile is equal to approximately 1.61 kilometers.

**Pepper spray:** A chemical used to repel bears and other dangerous creatures. It causes irritation and burning to the skin and eyes.

**Poaching:** The act of harvesting an animal at a time and place where it is illegal. Always follow the local hunting laws and regulations.

**Process a kill:** This is when an animal is butchered and cut up into pieces of meat to prepare for cooking. A kill can be processed by yourself or commercially.

**Prey:** Animals that are hunted for food—either by humans or other animals. It can also mean the act of hunting.

**Roosting:** What birds do when they rest upon a branch or a tree. Roosting keeps sleeping birds safe from predators.

**Scout:** To look ahead and observe an area. It is important to scout an area before hunting there. It helps you find evidence of your prey.

**Suburbia:** The area, people, and culture of a suburban, which is an area outside of a city or town where people live. It is often a small area full of houses.

**Swamp:** An area of wet land covered in grasses, trees, and other plant life. A swamp is not a good place to build a home, but it can be a good place to hunt.

**Thicket:** A collection of bushes and branches where small animals, like rabbits and rodents, like to hide.

**Timid:** A lack of confidence; shy. Rabbits, deer, and birds are often timid, which helps keep them alert and safe from predators.

**Vegetation:** All of the plant life in an area.

# INDEX

squirrels, 33, 36
See also nuisance animals
stamina, 6, 13
stance, 62
starter fuel. See kindling
summer camps, 69
survival kits, 53
See also bushcraft
survival skills. See bushcraft

**T**
target practice, 58–70
tent, 7, 16
toiletries, 16
tracking, 34–35
traps
advantages of, 27
assorted, 27fig
and bait, 33
bait for, 33–34
foot-hold, 29, 30fig
hunting journal, 65
live, 26, 28fig, 29
and nuisance animals, 36
safety with, 30–32
scouting before using, 34–36
trivia
Daniel Boone, 70
Ernest Hemingway, 22–23
examples of surviving, 54–55
fur trapping, 37–38

**W**
water, 7, 17, 19
waterproof bag, 17–18
waterproof matches, 44
weapons, 59–61, 68
wet weather, 10, 12
wildlife, 41

## FURTHER READING

Miles, Justin. *Ultimate Mapping Guide for Kids*. Firefly Books. 2016.

Colson, Rob. *Ultimate Survival Guide for Kids*. Firefly Books. 2015.

Long, Denise. *Survival Kid: A Practiced Guide to Wilderness Survival*. Chicago Review Press. 2011.

Livingston, Eustace Hazard. *The Trapper's Bible: The Most Complete Guide on Trapping and Hunting Tips Ever*. Skyhorse Publishing. 2012.

Brennan, Stephen. *Mountain Man Skills: Hunting, Trapping, Woodworking, and More*. Skyhorse Publishing 2015.

## INTERNET RESOURCES

https://www.outdoorlife.com/photos/gallery/survival/2013/03/how-build-trap-15-best-survival-traps/
An excellent article from Outdoor Life magazine that contains some good pictures and descriptions on handmade traps you can easily construct.

http://www.bsatroop780.org/skills/AllSkills.html
This website is run by the Boy Scouts and it contains lots of useful information on camping skills.

http://www.dec.ny.gov/docs/administration_pdf/0412survival.pdf
This site has great info on what to pack for a trip into the wilderness and how to assemble a survival kit.

http://wdfw.wa.gov/living/nuisance/trapping.html
Very good information on trapping animals using live traps. Also, good info dealing with the times not to trap an animal.

http://wildlife.ohiodnr.gov
This website contains valuable info on hunting and traffic basics.

# ORGANIZATIONS TO CONTACT

## The National Shooting Sports Foundation
Flintlock Ridge Office Center
11 Mile Hill Road
Newton, CT 06470-2359
Phone: (203) 426-1320
Fax: (203) 426-1087
Internet: https://www.nssf.org/

## National Firearms Association
P.O. Box 49090
Edmonton, Alberta
Canada T6E 6H4
Phone: 1-877-818-0393
Fax: 780-439-4091
Internet: https://nfa.ca

## The International Hunter Education Association
800 East 73rd Ave, Unit 2
Denver, Co 80229
Phone: 303-430-7233
Fax: 303-430-7236
Internet: https://www.ihea-usa.org

## The National Wildlife Federation
11100 Wildlife Center Drive
Reston, VA 20190
Phone: 1-800-822-9919
Internet: https://www.nwf.org

# PHOTO CREDITS

Page: 1: Pavel Rodimov | Dreamstime.com; 3: Alexei Novikov | Dreamstime.com; 6: Alys | Dreamstime.com; 7: Everst | Dreamstime.com; 8: Peter Lewis | Dreamstime.com; 9: Ocskay Bence | Dreamstime.com; 11(Top Photo): Loganban | Dreamstime.com; 11(Bottom Photo): Sander Van Der Werf | Dreamstime.com; 13: Teerawat Winyarat | Dreamstime.com; 14: Lauren Pretorius | Dreamstime.com; 15: defotoberg / Shutterstock.com; 16: Paweł Gubernat | Dreamstime.com; 17: Akaphat Porntepkasemsan | Dreamstime.com; 19: Mikołaj Tomczak | Dreamstime.com; 21: Steven Cukrov | Dreamstime.com; 22: Justinhoffmanoutdoors | Dreamstime.com; 24: Rschnaible | Dreamstime.com; 25: Charles Lytton | Dreamstime.com; 26: Sgoodwin4813 | Dreamstime.com; 28: Eutoch | Dreamstime.com; 29: Pablo Hidalgo | Dreamstime.com; 30: Tatisoroka | Dreamstime.com; 31: Steve Byland | Dreamstime.com; 33: Denis Trofimov | Dreamstime.com; 35: Peter Marble | Dreamstime.com; 36: stocksolutions / Shutterstock.com; 38: Benjamin Haas | Dreamstime.com; 39: Bazruh | Dreamstime.com; 40; Yordan Nedialkov | Dreamstime.com; 42: Sonofabear | Dreamstime.com; 43: Snyfer | Dreamstime.com; 44: Kushnirov Avraham | Dreamstime.com; 45: Amelia Martin | Dreamstime.com; 46: Prillfoto | Dreamstime.com; 47: Splendens | Dreamstime.com; 48: Bellemedia | Dreamstime.com; 50: Brad Calkins | Dreamstime.com; 52: Sergei Kazakov | Dreamstime.com; 54: Marlee | Dreamstime.com; 55: Teresa Kenney | Dreamstime.com; 56: Chris Johnson | Dreamstime.com; 58: Bonita Cheshier | Dreamstime.com; 59: Alexei Novikov | Dreamstime.com; 60: Dreamstime Agency | Dreamstime.com; 61: Vlue | Dreamstime.com; 62: Djtaylor | Dreamstime.com; 64: Georgios Kollidas | Dreamstime.com;

Background image: DaGa5 / Shutterstock.com

Cover photo: Design Pics Inc / Alamy Stock Photo

# VIDEO CREDITS

## Chapter 1
This video shows how to use a stick and the sun to tell directions:
http://x-qr.net/1HNV

## Chapter 2
How to Set a Cage Trap for Raccoons and Opossums: http://x-qr.net/1EQi

## Chapter 3
This Swiss video shows a lot of useful bushcraft techniques, such as using wedges of wood to split logs and make kindling and how to start a fire for cooking and warmth. http://x-qr.net/1HEg

## Chapter 4
This short video from the National Shooting Sports Foundation covers firearm safety and etiquette at the indoor shooting range: http://x-qr.net/1EJ2

## AUTHOR'S BIOGRAPHY

Elizabeth Dee has hunted extensively in the southeast part of the United States for small and large game. She has also cleaned and cooked game for family meals. Elizabeth has been writing for over 25 years for magazines and web articles.